Clancy of The Overflow

A. B. "BANJO" PATERSON

Illustrated by Evert Ploeg

ANGUS
& ROBERTSON
PUBLISHERS

I had written him a letter which I had, for want of better
    Knowledge, sent to where I met him down the Lachlan, years ago;
He was shearing when I knew him, so I sent the letter to him,
    Just "on spec", addressed as follows: "Clancy, of The Overflow".

And an answer came directed in a writing unexpected,
    (And I think the same was written with a thumbnail dipped in tar);
'Twas his shearing mate who wrote it, and *verbatim* I will quote it:
    "Clancy's gone to Queensland droving, and we don't know where he are."

In my wild erratic fancy visions come to me of Clancy
    Gone a-droving "down the Cooper" where the Western drovers go;
As the stock are slowly stringing, Clancy rides behind them singing,
    For the drover's life has pleasures that the townsfolk never know.

And the bush hath friends to meet him, and their kindly voices greet him
In the murmur of the breezes and the river on its bars,

And he sees the vision splendid of the sunlit plains extended,
And at night the wondrous glory of the everlasting stars.

I am sitting in my dingy little office, where a stingy
    Ray of sunlight struggles feebly down between the houses tall,
And the foetid air and gritty of the dusty, dirty city
    Through the open window floating, spreads its foulness over all.

And in place of lowing cattle, I can hear the fiendish rattle
Of the tramways and the buses making hurry down the street,

And the language uninviting of the gutter children fighting,
  Comes fitfully and faintly through the ceaseless tramp of feet.

And the hurrying people daunt me, and their pallid faces haunt me
As they shoulder one another in their rush and nervous haste,
With their eager eyes and greedy, and their stunted forms and weedy,
For townsfolk have no time to grow, they have no time to waste.

And I somehow rather fancy that I'd like to change with Clancy,
   Like to take a turn at droving where the seasons come and go,

While he faced the round eternal of the cashbook and the journal —
But I doubt he'd suit the office, Clancy, of "The Overflow".

ANGUS & ROBERTSON PUBLISHERS

Unit 4, Eden Park, 31 Waterloo Road,
North Ryde, NSW, Australia 2113;
94 Newton Road, Auckland 1,
New Zealand; and
16 Golden Square, London W1R 4BN,
United Kingdom

First published in Australia
by Angus & Robertson Publishers in 1989
First published in New Zealand
by Angus & Robertson NZ Ltd in 1989

"Clancy of the Overflow" by A. B. Paterson:
copyright reserved — proprietor Retusa Pty Ltd

Illustrations copyright © Evert Ploeg 1989

National Library of Australia
Cataloguing-in-publication data.

Paterson, A. B. (Andrew Barton), 1864-1941.
   Clancy of the Overflow.
   ISBN 0 207 16198 4.
   I. Ploeg, Evert. II. Title.
A821'.2

Typeset in 14pt Century Oldstyle by The Typeshop Pty Ltd
Printed in Singapore